The Love of Mortal Beings

The Love of Mortal Beings

by

Batnadiv HaKarmi

© 2023 Batnadiv HaKarmi-Weinberg. All rights reserved.
This material may not be reproduced in any form, published,
reprinted, recorded, performed, broadcast,
rewritten or redistributed without
the explicit permission of Batnadiv HaKarmi-Weinberg.
All such actions are strictly prohibited by law.

Cover design by Shay Culligan
Cover image *Untitled,* by Caron Greenblatt, 2021
Author photo by Netanel Cohen, 2023

ISBN: 978-1-63980-292-0

Kelsay Books
502 South 1040 East, A-119
American Fork, Utah 84003
Kelsaybooks.com

For my grandparents,
חיים יעקב בן בנימין משה
שמחה פריידל בת חיים אריה לייב
ת'נ'צ'ב'ה
May their souls be bound in the bond of life

Acknowledgments

I would like to thank Marcela Sulak, whose class on documentary poetry gave me the courage and tools to begin writing down the family history that had been haunting me since my grandparents' death, and to thank Linda Zisquit for encouraging me to write through the framework of myth.

Many thanks to my friends-in-poetry Geula Geurts, Margy Kerr-Jarrett, and Sarah Sassoon, for feedback and encouragement along the way. It was Geula who suggested the title for this book.

Thank you to Karen Kelsay and the amazing staff at Kelsay Books for getting this book out into the world—and for their patience as I navigated late pregnancy, birth, and postpartum fog.

I am grateful to the editors and staff of the following publications, in which some of these poems appeared, at times in earlier versions:

Arc Poetry Magazine: "Questions I never asked my grandfather"
Cumberland River Review: "When my grandmother was Rachel"
Flash Fiction Boulevard: "Shalom"
Poetry Super Highway: "Intermittent Fasting"

A special thank you to Caron Greenblatt for the use of her beautiful painting as the cover image of this book.

Contents

My grandmother looks back	11
Questions I Never Asked My Grandfather	12
Our Daily Bread	14
Waste not, want	16
When my grandfather was Abram	17
Bubby's Calendar	19
When my grandfather was Isaac	20
Who Knows One?	21
When my grandfather was Jacob	23
Stealing the Birthright	24
Reasons I Write About My Grandmother	27
When my grandmother was Rachel	29
My Grandmother Searches for Joseph	30
When my grandmother was the Witch of En-Dor	31
Shalom	33
Intermittent Fasting	36
My Grandmother and King Saul	38
When my grandfather was David	40
Confessional	42

My grandmother looks back

look not behind thee . . .
lest thou be consumed
　　　　—Genesis 19:17

The angel said not to.
But angels are not to be trusted—

they're all mission and disguises—
and the dead do come back

her own father returned as a beggar
crouched outside the station door.

Her husband runs ahead
arms swinging. Easy

to move when his body never
sank with the weight

of another's being; to float
when a salt sea never

splashed in his belly.
So easy, not to look

with no cord stretched taught—
bleeding, yet refusing to rupture.

Look not, say the angels
yet who will bear witness?

Who will count the burning windows,
and subtract them one by one?

Questions I Never Asked My Grandfather

I never asked your brothers' names.
I never asked their ages.
I never asked if there were three or four—
    in that one picture, it looks like four.
I never asked if you still hoped
as you fled across the Siberian plains.
I never asked when you knew they were gone.
I know when they died.
I know where they lie.
I know you never wanted to return.
I never asked how it felt, to cross those plowed fields.
If the earth grabbed your feet.
I didn't ask how the air smelled. *It was so green,* you said.
Never asked what you murmured as you sat on that ledge.
I know the earth sank, as though they dragged it from within.
I never asked if you spoke to them.
If you felt them stir.
I know you would not eat the plants nor drink the water of that
    place.
I never asked what Ella looked like.
An only girl. So sweet.
Didn't ask if she too had red hair.
Never asked if she had a favorite brother,
if that favorite was you.
Never asked if you knew where she is buried.
I know the women were taken elsewhere.
Didn't asked if your mother was big-boned or small.
Never asked about the shape of her face.
I know her name. Hasya Miriam.
Know you insisted Hasya be my mother's name.
I never asked if it gave you comfort, to say your mother's name,
    again and again.

I know my mother's picture was the one by your bed.
Look at her smile, you said.
I never asked why you chose that photo.
If you looked at it, before you went to sleep.
Never asked who you saw, when I'd look up, and find you
    watching me intently.
Never asked if all that love was for me.

Our Daily Bread

Bubby sliced deliberately.
Knife in swollen palm,
she pressed down hard,
cut one identical piece
after another, saying
*Whenever my mother cut
bread, she cried—
she knew that tomorrow
we'd be hungry. She knew
she should say no—
but couldn't, so cut
till it was gone,
and all along, she cried.*
When the loaf was gone,
Bubby lay down the knife,
wiped it, said: *One time,
only one time, my mother
struck me. Always
she walked to the next town for rations.
One day, she said: today we will have cake.
She walked and walked,
then walked the whole way back.
There was no cake
just a small loaf of bread.
My brother and I, we say: We strike!
We thought we were so big
strike like all the workers.
No cake, no bread!
And my mother struck me.
Hand to her cheek.
The only time my mother struck me.*

And now she is crying,
as she realizes,
every time again,
it was her mother's bread-ration
she had refused to eat.

Waste not, want

The cracked cupboards
are stacked with airline dishes—
eat breakfast on Tower
or TWA divided trays
with cutlery that bends when you press.

Leftovers, covered with a plate
go in the fridge,
When food discolors,
Bubby cuts off the mold
and eats what is left.

Scraps that can't be eaten
are sorted to the three bags beneath the sink:
Big pieces for the deer;
middle sized for the *gatchkes;*
the crumbs are carefully swept
off the tablecloth for the *meratchkes.*

A doe and her fawn haunt the crabapple tree
where Bubby heaps the bread too old to toast.
At night, the geese hoot forlorn
in the distant pond. In the morning,
we drop them the crusts, one by one.
And the ants, knowing they will be fed
do not invade.

When my grandfather was Abram

And God said to Abram:
Get you from your country,
from your kindred,
from your father's house,
to a land that I will show you.
                —Genesis 12:1

When my grandfather left
his country, no one
showed the way.
He flipped through books, waited for signs
tried to trace the contours of God's face.

When my grandfather left
his kindred, he clung
to a train that snaked across plains,
crossed one border, then another.
Those who blessed him were not blessed;
those who cursed him, not cursed.

When my grandfather left
his father's house, he lost
his name. Buried
in false papers, famine
dogged his footsteps.

When my grandfather left
his kindred, he begged
his brothers to come.
They said: Don't go to a Godless place.
They said: Come back to your father's house.

When he left his father's house
my grandfather thought he would return.
But when he sent an elder student back
the well was a ditch beyond the fields
full of blood and bones.
No women remained to draw water.

When my grandfather came back
to his kindred, he sat
by the ditch and whispered.

The banks were green.
The earth was red.
He would drink no water.

Bubby's Calendar

Remember the seventh day
to sanctify it . . .
          —Exodus 20:8

She remembered the days,
marked them her own way.

Shabbos night sanctified
to the memory of her mother:
My mother was worn out.
Her eyes were always red.
But when she lit the Shabbos candles
my mama was so beautiful!
Why could no one see
my mama was zeyer shayn*?*

She wept as she entered the Succah:
The beginning of exile.
My papa was farshikt.
They came during Kiddush
took him away.

Pesach, the time of bondage:
They held bread under my nose, and said:
aren't you hungry?

Rosh Hashana. The day she judged.
I begged Him to take me in place of my son.
He refused.

Yom Kippur. The day she did not forgive.

When my grandfather was Isaac

his father didn't take him to Moriah—
he made his way alone.
He carried the bindings and the wood.
He carried his friend.
Sometimes he stopped to ask,
Where is the lamb?

When my grandfather was Isaac,
he looked for a hilltop
lit by fire, looked for an angel
with arm outstretched, crying *stop*.
The iced tundra was endless and flat.

When my grandfather climbed the altar
he held himself down
with the weight of his friend's wasted body.
He hollowed himself with hunger.
He didn't hear the angel call.
He left his ashes gathered
to mark the place.

Who Knows One?

Bubby knows one.
One was the time her mother hit her.
> *She said she'd bring cake,*
> *but she brought bread.*
> *We said: "we strike!"*
> *And my mama struck me.*

Who knows two?
Bubby knows two.
Two are the brothers killed.
> One by the *Einsatzgruppen*
> One in Leningrad.

Three are the sons.
Take away one.

Four are the brothers.
> One escaped,
> one missing,
> two dead.

Five are the kilometers her mother walked for rations.
Five are the kilometers she walked back.

Six are the years her father was *gennomen*,
a gnomon, gone.

Who knows seven?
Bubby knows seven.
Seven are the months in Moscow,
watching her mother die.

Eight are the hours in labor
before her husband realized he should come.

Nine are the months she carried her son.

Eleven are the months she outlived him.

Bubby knows the mediums of exchange,
a system of weights
in which she is always found wanting.

Who teaches you to divide and subtract?
Bubby hovers
over your shoulder, to mark each mistake.

When my grandfather was Jacob

he stole the birthright from my grandmother.
He didn't mean to—
but he loved his mother,
and my grandmother was so tired, unto death.

He knew the right to the firstborn's
name goes to the mother.
"Let's split it," he said,
with nothing to barter.
"Half of your mother,
half of mine."

She refused.
He took.
He knew, even then, a thief is fined twice—
a fee he could not pay
a fury he could not flee.

Stealing the Birthright

The Rabbi told him not to do it: "It belongs to the mother. Let her name the child."
Zaidy said, "But who knows if I'll have another."
The Rabbi said, "I bless you that you will have another daughter. Let your wife have the name."
Zaidy sat silent. He seemed to be listening. He always did as he was told.

When Rebbetzin Bloch said that the first birth goes slowly, that the baby would not be born for hours, he listened. He went to Yeshiva to *daven*. Bubby remained standing outside the Yeshiva door.

The debate began: How would she get to the hospital on Shabbos? Labor had just started. Should she walk? Call an ambulance?
The Rabbi still hovered. Pointing at his wife, he said, "You take her. *Now.*"
The debate stopped. Rebbetzin Bloch drove Bubby to the hospital.

Zaidy stayed in the Yeshiva through *Musaf.* They told him not to worry. It will take time. He listened, and stayed for *Kiddush,* then set off on foot.

"He always listened to what people told him, like a good little Yeshiva *bachur,*" my grandmother would say. "They said it goes slow, so he stayed for *Shaharis,* then Torah reading, then *Musaf, Kiddush,* herring and kugel."

My grandmother gave birth alone.

Holding her baby, all she wanted was to feed her. Fill her up, till she brimmed with milk, as Bubby had never been filled.
The nurses patiently explained to the ignorant immigrant that formula is much more sanitary, that it is scientifically designed to be healthy for babies.

Bubby was stubborn.
She found a doctor who spoke Russian and was also ignorant. He agreed to sneak her the baby.
She held the tiny creature she could not believe had come from her body, could not believe had nestled and turned in her shrunken belly. Even when Bubby had stretched herself over the Maharal's grave, begging for a child, she hadn't believed she would hold life in her hands.
She had starved for so long, she no longer menstruated. Now her body was dripping food.

The baby gripped her breast with five perfect fingers.
She remembered her mother's fingers as she lit the candles. How her swollen hands gleamed, suddenly beautiful.
"Mine," she thought. "Tziporah Hyena. My little bird brought to life." This was the one gift she could give her mother, abandoned in a beggar's grave at the outskirts of Moscow.

My grandfather finally arrived. He watched the small curled form in awe.
He remembered the last time he had seen his mother. It was right after his sister's wedding. As he prepared to return to Yeshiva, his mother had clung to him and cried.
"I'll be back," he assured her.
Four weeks later, she was dead, shot in the back by the *Einsatzgruppen*. He tried not to imagine the slow topple of her body into a ditch. In his mind, she was still clothed, gleaming in wedding finery. Sometimes he could feel her tears, stinging his dry eyes.
"Hasya Miriam," he crooned to the sleeping infant.
Hasya—God shows care. Miriam—who watched her brother as he floated on the waters. The hidden eyes that never gave up.

The Rabbi told him to give in. The Rabbi told him to let go. My grandfather always listened.

He could hear the echo of his mother weeping. All of Israel waited for Miriam in the desert. All of Israel sat in mourning when Miriam died. And look, God had showed his everlasting care in the little baby that guzzled from his wife.

"Let's split the name," he said. "She'll be both Tziporah and Hasya."
Bubby refused. She didn't believe in halves. Her beautiful baby, with her ten fingers, ten toes, her milky skin, was a perfect whole.
"It's dangerous to call down the destiny of those who died young," Zaidy tried. "Better to make a change. She should be neither fully one nor the other."
Bubby didn't want a change. She wanted her mother.

But it was Zaidy who went to the Yeshiva to give the name.
He stood before the Rabbi and congregation, and named his daughter: Tziporah Hasya.
The Rabbi told him not to do it.
This one time, he didn't listen.

The last thing he said to my mother: I should have let her have the name.

Reasons I Write About My Grandmother

Because I do not know if I blame you.
Because I don't know if there is "I" or "you."
Because every time we washed the dishes, you said:
"My mother was *usgemutchered.* She worked so hard, and the water
    was frozen. Her hands were cracked, and red, and ruined."
Because as I dried, I looked at your hands, veined and swollen like
    a boxer's burst glove
and you cried: "But when my mother lit the candles, she was so
    beautiful."
Because in my mind, she was beautiful.
Because when I write these lines, my eyes grow wet.
Because you made my mother cry.
You knew how to press exactly where it hurt.
Because you once downed a whole bottle of aspirin with a glass of
    vodka.
I can imagine you, swallowing pill after pill, not looking at what
    your hands did.
Because you ate like clockwork, hand rising to mouth, eyes trained
    ahead.
You cut the mold off a graying piece of chicken and kept chewing.
Because I stayed in the hospital room when they changed you.
I thought it was love.
Because when you gripped my hands,
you were telling me to leave.
Because I rushed you to Yeshiva in a wheelchair for shofar.
I shamed you.
Because when Zaidy came to meet the ambulance
you turned your face away.
Because you never forgave.
I want to let go.
I want to hold on.
Because you never let go.

You erected a tombstone, even though they had no grave.
You cried every time your brothers' names were mentioned.
Because when you were finally reunited with one lost brother, your run was a hobble, your eyes were a river, the arrivals hall disappeared, it was just the two of you, forty years obliterated with your steps.
Because you spoke of your mother every time you lit the candles.
Because you sobbed every time you saw your sick son.
Because you had an indictment drawn up for your meeting with the Almighty.
Because you listed King Saul on it.
Because you went down to *She'ol* in mourning.

When I read that Jacob wouldn't be comforted, I think of you.

When I read that Rachel weeps for her children, I think of you.

You will bend God Himself to your will.

When my grandmother was Rachel

*And she called his name Joseph
saying, God shall add to me another son.*
                              —Genesis 30:24

she named her ghost child "more"
and every babe she held in her arms
was more more more more more—

behind each name lurked another name
between her arms, the void. She knew
how easy it was to disappear. Her father

gone for seven years,
returned as someone else.
Voracious, she gorged

on mandrake root, communed
with the dead. Gulped
wells dry, only to cry them full again.

She turned her husband away. Buried
herself by the side of the road. Refused

to come home, as she climbed, step by step
to hammer at God's door.

My Grandmother Searches for Joseph

The child is not—
And I, wither will I go?
    —Genesis 37:30

Midnight, and Bubby is at the pit again
searching with a nightlight, though the child is gone—
She knows he's alive, for *there is no comfort for the loss*
of the living.

Midnight, and Bubby is at the closet again
seeking the coat of colors, though his smell is long gone.
He is surely devoured, his father says. She rubs at the stain till her
fingers bleed.

Midnight, and my grandmother is weeping again
She knows he is somewhere, even though he is gone.

When my grandmother was the Witch of En-Dor

Then said Saul unto his servants:
'Seek me a woman that divineth by a ghost,
that I may go to her, and inquire of her.'
      —I Samuel 28:7–8

Her pacing feet
dig a ditch
a cubit deep

Her fingers
incessant
shred inflamed skin.

The dead
are weak,
have forgotten how to speak.

Scattered shadows,
they dissipate
like smoke.

She squeezes blood
from flayed flesh
to call them close.

They perch on her back.
She croons
their names.

> *Tziporah Hyena*
> *Yosef Nehemya*
> *Yehuda Leib*

Half-ghosts
she also
grips by name

When her son lies dying
no one
will take her to him,

can't abide the screams,
    Shalom Yehuda.
But his wife says:

At least
when she's here
I remember who he is.

Shalom

1941
The fields speed by the window—so different from the narrow corridors connecting the walkup room she shared with her mother to the building-block's toilet and stove.
She arrives, and Shalom is unrecognizably bigger—baby-fat gone, head almost as high as her shoulder.
He doesn't ask about their mother, so she doesn't have to tell.
When she says she's come for him, he says, "Moscow is no place for a *yiddishe bachur*. I'll be Bar Mitzva soon."

1945
She has her sister, and her father has been released. She tells herself: be grateful; she tries to tell herself: this is enough. As they cross the Ural Mountains, she tells herself: a child wouldn't make it. Then she remembers he would be sixteen by now.

1948
She cups her hand round her belly, tries to feel the heartbeat, imagines the face, floating in its watery moon.
Whose soul will she call down? Eliyah is alive, thank God—he sent a message from Israel; Yoska is missing, but who knows; Shmul Modkheh, killed on the last day of Leningrad; and Shalom—her mind flinches away—shot through the head by the *Einsatzgruppen*, who invaded the village only weeks after she left.
In the end, the baby is a girl.

1952
This time it's a boy.
"We'll name him Shalom," she says, looking at the still, sleeping face.
"Give another name," her husband urges. "Don't call down an evil fate."
She tags on Yehuda, but knows he is Shalom.

1956
He loves to watch the trains roar by at night. In the morning, they go to gather the metal pegs that sometimes loosen from the tracks. He is small, and wiry, and dark haired. She can't remember if her brother looked like that.

1960
She is making toast—more than a decade, and she still wonders at the bread's fleshy softness.
"After my father was taken away, I had to scatter the family," she tries to explain, "my mama—she had something growing in her brain."
He watches with uncomprehending eyes.
In some dreams, she's taken Shalom with her, and he's sitting with their mother, who is crying, "why did you bring him," crying, "he can't see me like this," and all she wants to say is, "Mama, you are beautiful."

1964
They are at the train station, watching boys congregate from all directions, dragging suitcases in preparation for the new *zman*.
In her head, the scene has played so many times: sometimes she grabs him and he kicks her away, runs down the path, past the village, and is saved by the forest; sometimes she drags him onto the train, and he's back with her in Moscow, the streets are dark, a soldier asks for papers, and Shalom again is gone; sometimes he's in their rented rooms, begging for their mother; sometimes they are by the grave, and he looks at her accusingly for abandoning their mother in this thicket of bones.
Shalom Yehuda cries that she is hurting him, breaks his arm free with a twelve-year-old's impatience.

1968
She waves and waves as the train sets off—he is already talking to his friends, and doesn't notice. Tears trail down her cheeks unchecked. How old would he be now, if she hadn't cried, turned around, and gotten back on that train?
There, that dark haired man there—it could be him.

1972
He fell down during *Shaharit,* flat on the floor. The rabbi sent him home.
Now he is wrapped in a sheet, dark hair shaved in front, the doctor holds a scalpel, and he will cut into the skull, try to exorcise the tumor burrowed in the brain.
She wonders where the bullet hit, as she swallows pill after pill.

Intermittent Fasting

Eat, my grandfather cajoled my mother
every fast day but Yom Kippur.

Forbid fasting if she was pregnant or nursing.
Believed that mothers of young children
must always be filled.

You fast, she said.
I am old, he said.

He had starved long enough
to see no holiness in lack

yet fasted Monday and Thursday
and Monday again. Kept
the ancient abstinence

with trudging care.
Penance for living.

The bachurim, his wife accused.
The bachurim—the yeshiva boys in his care

who turned back at the border
while he continued and crossed.

Their death is on you, she said.
She saw ghosts everywhere.

Said this was the reason their son fell.
Couldn't speak.
Would have no children.

My grandfather soundlessly
swallowed the blame.

Dragged it as he bore
his friend across the Siberian planes.

Returned to hunger,
the taste of grass.

Hollowed himself
to hold their names.

My Grandmother and King Saul

And when Saul inquired of the Lord,
the Lord answered him not,
neither by dreams, nor by Urim, nor by prophets . . .
And Saul . . . came to the woman by night; and said:
'Divine unto me, I pray thee, by a ghost,
and bring me up whomsoever I shall name unto thee.'
                              —I Samuel 28:6–8

"It's not right," my grandmother would say
"what God did to Saul.
Ich bein fun Shaul HaMelekh—
I feel it! I feel it!
He was a good man.
He didn't want to be king.
Look what happened to him."

When the dark bird
circled Saul
she stood with a carpet to chase it away.
A sturdy scarecrow in a white turban and faded housedress—
she didn't believe in singing
and had never liked redheads.

When he came searching for the dead
because there was no one alive
left to call on
she fed him *fayn couchin* and schnitzel,
sliced chicken liver to slivers as she wept—
she could lasso the dead
by the neck
and yank them up
with the sound of that weeping.

She told Saul not to worry.
She crooned, Love, one more day,
and it will all be over.

It can never hurt as much, down there—
and your son—
he will be with you.

When my grandfather was David

*David besought God for the child; and David fasted,
and . . . lay all night upon the earth.
He said, 'While the child was yet alive,
I fasted and wept
I said, "Who can tell whether God will be gracious to me,
that the child may live?"
But now he is dead; why should I fast?
Can I bring him back again?
I shall go to him, but he shall not return to me.'*
—II Samuel 12:16–22

he sat for hours by his son's bed.
He held the slack hand.
He said, over and over again:
*"The salvation of God
is like the blink of an eye.
Say it!"*
But his son could not speak.

When my grandfather was David,
he sang sweetly
to banish the evil spirit
circling his son's bed,
*"There is kindness in God,
for we are not annihilated.
His mercy has not ended."*
He moved the paralyzed hand up and down.

When he saw his son
could no longer blink,
could no longer stir to music,
could feel only pain,
my grandfather gently laid the limp hand to rest.
He prayed for mercy.

His son drifted into dark sleep.
My grandfather kissed him goodbye.
My grandmother turned her face away
and wept herself to death.

When my grandfather was David
he went to *she'ol* to his son.
Their bodies mingled in the soft soil.
He engraved his father's name on the tombstone,
so he would hear him rustling above.

Confessional

After Frank Bidart

Is she dead?
Yes, she is dead.
Did you forgive her?
What is there to forgive?
Did she forgive you?
No, she did not forgive me.
What did you have to forgive?
She was wild. Cruel sometimes,
almost unwilled.
A mess of loving.

When our son lay beneath the knife
she swallowed her own poison.
We found her on the floor.

She was wholly consumed
with the love of
MORTAL BEINGS—

Did you forgive her?
When she got out of the hospital,

she said NOTHING . . .

but she didn't try to die
again. She accepted GOD
       wanted her to live.

If she was Abraham,
she would have climbed onto the altar

would have slit her own throat
       not looking for a ram.

But when you try to switch a sacrifice
> *both it and the change thereof shall be holy;*
> *it shall not be redeemed.*

Did you forgive her?
"O Absalom, Absalom my son
would I had died in your place
Absalom my son"
David's inconsolable scream.

Yet she hurt
      our daughters . . .

Did you forgive her?
After he died,
she willed herself to die.
She did not make his first *yahrzeit*.

Standing over her shrouded
form I realized
her anger still lived—

      Over and over
I reviewed our life, every crime
every slight, every slip I had made.

The name I stole,
the furniture I never bought . . .

It was then
I finally said to her,
      Whatever you want!
      Whatever you want!
I *did* love her.

What did she have to forgive?
I took her
to exile.

      She dreamed of Israel
and I—

I RAN AS FAST AS I COULD TO THE NEW TELZ.

I thought I could retrieve
the lost,
dragged her
to join the remnants
of Lithuania in the new yeshiva.

Did she forgive you?
She didn't fit in.
Burning eyes,
perfect Russian.
Tolstoy for breakfast.

Did she forgive you?
I bought two plots in Jerusalem.

She shut the blinds,
      like she was trying to shut out the street.

Told me
"If I don't make it there living
I won't go there dead."

I heard her speak to the grandchildren
about renting a room
alone
in Jerusalem,
earning her right to stay.

Her heart faltered.

When she came back
      from the hospital—
I ran to greet her.

SHE TURNED HER FACE AWAY.

I knew then
she *wouldn't* forgive me . . .

Did you forgive her?
After she died, I found notes, littered
all around the house.
She left her will for everyone to find:

She demanded to be buried in Cleveland.
She did not want the funeral to be
in the Yeshiva.
She wanted to be buried
in the pauper's cemetery.
She would not be buried beside me.

A pile of notes . . .
her cupboard, the bathroom, the closet.
I could have burned them . . .
I could have ignored them.
The children hoped I would.

But I thought:
will this give me ABSOLUTION?

If I finally listen.
If I let this "mortal being"
choose?

I did as she asked.
We drove from the house for an hour and a half
all the way to the old *Hesed Shel Emet* cemetery.
I buried her in the pauper's graveyard.
I ignored the questions—
she always said I cared too much
what the Telzers thought.

Did she forgive you?
By the end of the *shiva,*
a new legend was born—
People said: it was a mark of the Rebbetzin's compassion,
how she always cried with the needy
and now threw her lot in with them.
They said it was a sign of her modesty.

She had become a saint in her own right.

Notes

When my grandfather was Abram
"those who blessed him were not blessed . . . ."—inverts Genesis 12:3.
"When he sent an elder student back . . ."—alludes to Genesis 24, where Abraham sends his "elder servant" back to his homeland in order to seek a bride for Isaac. The servant finds this bride by the town well.

Bubby's Calendar
Pesach is the Jewish holiday of freedom, commemorating the exodus from bondage in Egypt.
Succot, the "Holiday of Booths," commemorates the years of wandering in the desert. Traditionally, it is also seen as enacting a mini-exile to atone for sins that might have been recalled on Rosh Hashana, the Jewish New Year and Day of Judgment.
Yom Kippur is the "Day of Atonement," on which God forgives all wrongdoing that is not interpersonal.

When my grandfather was Isaac alludes to the Binding of Isaac, Genesis 22.
"He left his ashes gathered to mark the place"—adapted from Babylonian Talmud, Tractate Zevachim, 62b: "How did the [returnees from the Babylonian Exile] know the proper location of the altar? [. . .] They saw the ashes of Isaac gathered in that place."

"Who knows one?" is a Jewish folk song included in the Passover Haggadah, and traditionally sung at the Seder. The song has versions in Yiddish and Judeo-Arabic, as well as many other Jewish dialects.

When my grandfather was Jacob intertwines the story of Jacob's purchase of the birthright from Esau in Genesis 25, and Jacob's theft of Esau's blessing at his mother's command in Genesis 27.
"tired, unto death"—from Genesis 25:29, 32.

"a thief is fined twice"—from Exodus 22:4: "If a man delivers to his friend money or articles to keep, and it is stolen out of the man's house, if the thief is found, he shall pay double."

Stealing the Birthright
"How would she get to the hospital on Shabbos?"—It is forbidden to use a car on the Jewish Sabbath, except in cases of *Pikuach Nefesh* (lit. 'watching over a soul'*)* where doing so might help preserve human life. The Talmud rules that any action undertaken to help a woman who is giving birth falls into this category.
"Tziporah"—Heb. "bird."
"*Einsatzgruppen*" were SS paramilitary death squads that were responsible for mass murder, primarily by shooting, during World War II in German-occupied Europe. In the early stages of the implementation of the "Final Solution to the Jewish question," these units were responsible for liquidating the Jewish populations in conquered territory. It is estimated they killed around 1.3 million Jews before the Nazis decided to move to the use of gas in order to conserve bullets.
"Hasya"—Heb. "God (*ya*) shows care (*has*)."

Reasons I Write about My Grandmother
"Shofar"—blowing the shofar horn is the centerpiece of Rosh Hashana services, and the culmination of the prayer service on Yom Kippur.
"When I read the Jacob wouldn't be comforted"—in Genesis 37:25: "he refused to be comforted, saying 'I shall go down to *She'ol* to my son in mourning.'"
"When I read that Rachel weep for her children"—in Jeremiah 31:15: "A voice was heard in Ramah, lamentation and bitter weeping, Rachel weeping for her children, refusing to be comforted, for her children are not."
"bend God himself to your will"—allusion to Rachel's rebuke of God in *Tanna Debei Eliyahu Rabbah,* 30:1.

When my grandmother was Rachel
"she named her ghost child 'more'"—from Genesis 30:24, where Rachel names her first born son "Yosef" (lit. 'increase' or 'more').
"seven years"—an allusion to the seven years Jacob labors to earn the right to marry Rachel (Genesis 29:20).
"returned as someone else"—an allusion to Genesis 29:25, where Rachel's father replaces her with her sister Leah. Jacob awakes after his wedding night, "and behold, it is Leah."
"Gorged on mandrake root"—from Genesis 30:14.
"cry them full again"—alludes to Jeremiah 31:15.
"Buried herself by the side of the road"—from Genesis 48:7.

My Grandmother Searches for Joseph
"at the pit"—from Genesis 37:24: "and they took [Joseph] and cast him in a pit."
"*there is no comfort for the loss of the living*"—from Genesis Rabba 84:21: "*[Jacob] refused to be comforted* [. . .] for one is comforted for the [loss of the] dead, but there is no comfort [for the loss] of those who are still living."
"*He is surely devoured*"—from Genesis 37:34: "it is my son's coat. An evil beast hast surely devoured him . . ."

Shalom
"*zman*"—a Yeshiva semester.
"*Shaharit*"—morning prayers.

My Grandmother and King Saul
"*Ich bein fun Shaul HaMelekh*"—Yid. "I come from King Saul."
"When the dark bird / circled"—mixed allusion to I Samuel 16 and II Samuel 21:10.

When my grandfather was David
"he sang sweetly"—from I Samuel 16:23.
"*There is kindness in God*"—from Lamentations 3:22.

Confessional
"If she was Abraham"—alludes to the Binding of Isaac, Genesis 22.
"*both it and the change thereof shall be holy*"—from Leviticus 27:33.
"O Absalom, Absalom my son"—from II Samuel 18:33.

About the Author

Batnadiv HaKarmi's work has appeared in numerous literary journals, among them the *Ilanot Review, Arc Poetry Magazine, Rogue Agent,* and *Belmont Story Review*. Her biography of Holocaust rescue activist, Pinchas Rosenbaum, is upcoming from Gefen Publishing.

A writer and visual artist, Batnadiv studied painting at the New York Studio School, and holds an MA in Creative Writing from Bar Ilan University. She is the recipient of the Andrea Moriah Poetry Prize, and was shortlisted for the Brideport Prize for flash fiction, and Harbor Review's Jewish Women's Poetry Prize. Born in Stanford, California, she grew up in Jerusalem, where she currently resides with her husband and four young children.

www.ingramcontent.com/pod-product-compliance
Lightning Source LLC
Chambersburg PA
CBHW030917170426
43193CB00009BA/884